Heart Speaks, Is Spoken For

Heart Speaks, Is Spoken For

poetry by
Marjorie Maddox

photography by
Karen Elias

SHANTI ARTS PUBLISHING
BRUNSWICK, MAINE

Heart Speaks, Is Spoken For

Published by Shanti Arts Publishing
Interior and cover design by Shanti Arts Designs

Shanti Arts LLC
193 Hillside Road
Brunswick, Maine 04011
shantiarts.com

Printed in the United States of America

ISBN: 978-1-956056-06-8 (softcover)

Library of Congress Control Number: 2021946487

Contents

Acknowledgments

About Place: Works of Resistance and Resilience: "Memorial for George Floyd in Black and White" and *Memorial for George Floyd in Black and White*

Ars Medica: "Transplanted" and *Heart Speaks, Is Spoken For*

Black Moon Magazine: "Sepia" and *Heart Tree*

The Coop: A Poetry Cooperative: "Day Is Done. Is Beginning." and *Two Hearts*

The Cresset: "Heart in a Box"

The Ekphrastic Review: "Treacherous Driving" and *Snow Heart;* "Bury Our Heart" and *Fractured Heart*

Lily Poetry Review: "Chopping Block"

Masque & Spectacle: "Mourning Song for the Earth" and *Mourning Song for the Earth*

Open: Journal of Arts and Letters: "Heart, Lichen, Stone" and *Heart Holding On*

The Other Journal: "The Long and Winding Road" and *Asphalt Heart*

Perpendicular As I (Sandstone Poetry Book Award, 1994): "Chiromancy"

Transplant, Transport, Transubstantiation (Yellowglen Prize, WordTech Editions, 2004; Wipf and Stock, 2018): "Bury Our Heart," "Disconnected," and "Treacherous Driving"

Williamsport Living: "Treacherous Driving" and *Snow Heart*

Preface

Art inspires art.

Each angle, each image, each word enlarges meaning. We found this especially true while collaborating. Individual visions resonate one with the other to create a third, more expansive view.

In *Heart Speaks, Is Spoken For*, a cracked, heart-shaped stone inspired us to nuanced portrayals of love, obsession, grief, joy, loneliness, independence, anger, protest, and hope. It led us back to memories and forward to our responsibility for the earth, to fairy tales—real and shattered—and to this complicated world in which many of us—with our fragile, courageous hearts—benefit from the shared visions of others. Please join us on this collaborative ekphrastic path, which—we hope—will lead you as well to new insights and creations.

Treacherous Driving

"It's as safe as traveling to work..."

—a cardiologist before performing a transplant

The first night of the blizzard
that stranger inched into Ohio.
Halfway through he skidded
into our snow-spackled lives.
His heart is buried
in my father,
who is buried.

This is the hole
in the stranger, in my father,
in my own cracked
chest, hail cupped in its cavity,
the aorta beginning to freeze.

All winter,
the weather preaches white
lies: fields blank of roads,
a curve straightened,
the even light of sky.

Tonight the breeze is all
icicles, banner-like
from the clouds. Nothing
is moveable
in this treacherous state.

Our wheels spin,
their rhythm: a breath
that pulls us
then stalls. The law

of the body, of the state,
cannot replace the chain
reaction, jackknifed lives,
hope piling into hope.

The man and his heart,
cold on an icy road,
warmed us for weeks
while winter, a clear blue thing,
wafted light.

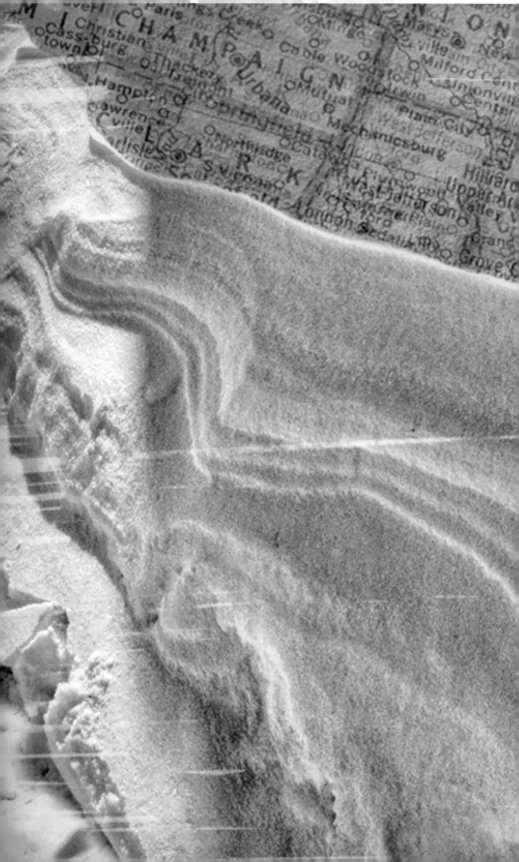

Snow Heart

Disconnected

*"The heart has its own nervous system . . .
[once transplanted, it] can beat
independently of the brain."*

—The Boston Globe Magazine

Its nerves left dangling,
so many severed cords
uncoiled and floundering
about un-insulated space
I think—until a priest-turned-
surgeon explains in stops and shocks
the transubstantiation of transplants,
what others' hearts were, are, continue to become
inside our opened hollows,
disconnected from used nerves
that bridge to blood.

Instead, this always-symbol,
always-physical of personage
completes itself, confidently connecting
to what it needs,
its sinoatrial node a part of
that separate chambered system
of someone else,
heart of the fact that keeps it still
believing what it does.

In the transplant waiting room,
a child asks her mother,
"Will Daddy love the same people?"
and I startle at the complications.

While the slow clock sterilizes
the lives of those waiting shock-still
or nervous-twitching,
I think, out-of-time, of persons whom I've become
on stage, transforming what I wasn't into
what I wasn't.

In seventh grade the penalty for breaking
character in Theater class was failure.
And so we sat obediently as old women,
but staring boldly, disconcertingly
back-and-forth at the blushing prop boy,
the unplugged cord, when,
in *Arsenic and Old Lace*,
the telephone kept ringing, ringing, ringing.

Disconnected

Its nerves left dangling,
so many severed cords
uncoiled and floundering . . .

Fractured Heart

Bury Our Heart

Like every other,
this is the year of shifting
sorrows, the thin shadows of land
that slip from countries we've left
for fear or want
of finding ourselves
in a handful of dirt.

Even in sleep,
a warm wonder of birth and loss,
there too the earth's vibrations,
the leveling of cliffs in eyes we claim.

The soul is the land
liquid in the lines of veins
that stripe the inner atlas.
It bubbles and flows, smoothes
the rough roads, carves out
our caves of refuge,
our weeping echoes.

Here too they will find us:
the outcasts, the fugitives,
the lost, the abandoned,
the running-for-our-lives.

O homeland of sadness,
these dusty bones that could not save.
I have held in my clay hands,
the fine grains of his blood,
bold in my muddy palms;
I have held in my earthen arms
the jagged pot of his pain,
brimming and bitter.

I have waited
for that open mouth
of the world
to lay him down.

Like every other,
this is the year of shifting
sorrows . . .

Transplanted

Though they'd never met,
the man with the dead man's heart
inside him dreamed his donor's
face, limbs, lungs; sung in his sleep
the dead man's favorite song
in the deep baritone voice
that wasn't his own but
his, the one not known or seen or heard,
except in night's deep cradle of sleep,
this stranger's metronome of a heart
humming behind ribs that no longer
felt like his—beautiful fence
for an organ lifted from someone else's
afterlife. Even waking, the new-
old man and his heart now know
nothing of old boundaries, the ones
composed by the living. Instead,
in bright, silent daylight,
he takes his first,
tentative beat
toward love.

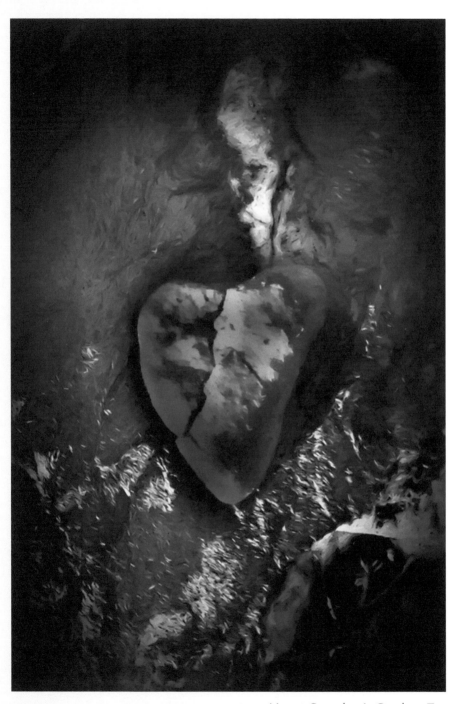

Heart Speaks, Is Spoken For

Chiromancy

Yes, I'd trace my own dark palm
for you, stretch this lifeline half a century,
cut it short. A bandanna tight on my head
like a tourniquet. Like a bandage bloodied from the Revolution.
Like a blindfold on a witch burning:
stake up the back, skirt flame-bright as a banshee or

quicker, neck split on a stone,
gold hoop glittering, you
on the other side of the knife,
face shaped by a black cloak,
mouth tauter than rope, tightening.

Maybe, one finger at a time, I'd slice,
save only my palm: small, smooth,
this curve here the curve of your cheek,
these lines the red in your eyes.

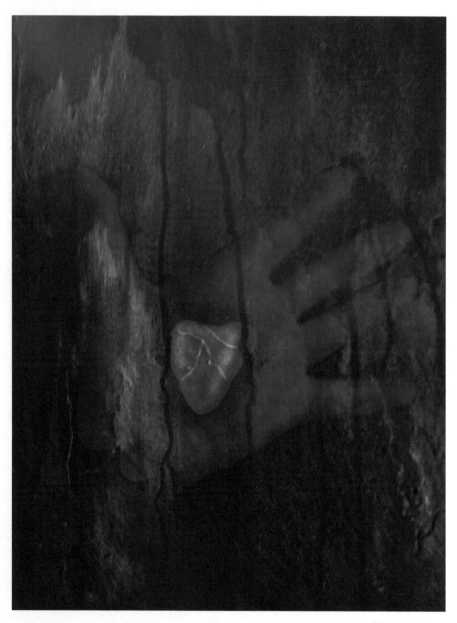

Heart Lines

Heart Waiting for Danger

Chopping Block

Always, the raised ax:
shattered sky, steel staring down
wood and victim. The danger

of waiting for danger
cracks us all, each swoop
of aim and blade decades

in the making. This is the way
of memory, its ringed age
circling the foundation of trunk,

snaking the blind heart,
each metal glint refracting
the angle of fear that grips

its evening ritual
of chop, chop, chop
while a stranger—someone

like you or me—lies shock-still, face up,
and crows, those dark bystanders,
caw-caw sharp warnings of light

and fairy tales gone bad, even now
darkening into never-after; into forest,
into trespass, into now.

Open your eyes and breathe.
The night creeps close on dead leaves.
The hunter swings again his sorrow. Flee.

Sepia

is the bare-tree
forest flight of Snow White
on a night when the hue
of every evil eye stalks
her ever-afters with envy
as twisted as any thicket
in this wilderness that scratches
and steals the tales
she once believed in

> is the Queen's bramble-
> thick commands the underling
> carries in each ear that won't
> hear and obey as his deadly
> axe swings its way instead
> to the neck of the ravenous
> boar circling her fear-
> blanched body

is the seed of mercy
when she finally sees
the forest *and* the trees,
the woodcutter and the woods,
the huntsman who refuses to hunt
her, no matter what the Mirror,
Mirror murmurs to the not
fairest of them all

is the seed of tree
that sprouts deliverance
when the silent trapper hauls
the heart heavy in his hands—
the heart not hers—back
to the heartless kingdom,
while she, lying beneath
the Mulberry's lacerated limb,

looks up to see
his tale is now engrained
with hers. The wind calls
and she tries to breathe—
not dwarfs and apples;
not coffins encasing
some predestined tale
of a prince wary of boars—

but something new,
unspoken. Remembering
the way the huntsman
swung his axe, she rises,
peers up past branches
to color and sky.
She climbs.
And you, reader,
climb with her.

Heart Tree

Asphalt Heart

The Long and Winding Road

No, no music but the heave
of your heart as you trudge

on this cracked-pavement
of a path that is your past

and future, the healing blisters
better than the gashed

memories that drip-drip-drip
Hansel-and-Gretel style

along this asphalt of survival,
which is some hope, yes,

that one-foot-in-front-of-the-other
platitude the real work of the living.

A road is a road is a road
leading somewhere not here

while each toe and heel dream
the unreal threshold: cool grasses,

still waters, glorious gates
of beautifully broken pearls.

Heart in a Box

—title of a CNN story featured on July 9, 2016

No picnic cooler look-alike, the kind
transporting a dead man's heart

to my father in '93 after his thirty
years of near-death when

the blizzard-driving really-
dead anonymous donor

said Yes to a life not his. No,
today's latest medical advance

keeps the dead's bloody
valentine pa-pa-pumming

all the way to the sterile
stretched-out-on-the-table almost-

corpse, knocked out while the crying
bystanders pray for mercy, for miracles,

and outside in the real bloody
world of Baton Rouge, Falcon Heights,

Dallas, my town/yours,
no heart pa-pa-pums

in Alton, Philandro, Lorne, Michael,
Brent, Patrick, Michael J.,

while waiting bystanders pray
for "advances" and "miracles."

And no heart pa-pa-pums in the dead-
silence of the dug-up ground

where they'll be transplanted,
bloody organs in another box,

because some said No
to a life not theirs,

while others—between the beats
and the beatings, the rat-a-tat-tats,

and the pa-pum, pa-pum, pa-pums—
tried to say Yes.

Remember Me

. . . today's latest medical advance
keeps the dead's bloody
valentine pa-pa-pumming

Memorial for George Floyd in Black and White

Memorial for George Floyd in Black and White
—Spring 2020

Cracked, gray-gone-dead:
the stone-cold heart pinned
by the pale blooms of buds
in this city that fences out
cherry blossoms and peace—
rubber bullets, pepper balls, smoke bombs,
all the unconstrained and uncalled for
on parade to a photo op across Lafayette Square
(its border street now renamed in bright caution yellow)—
to St. John's Episcopal where the everyday horror of now
is colorfully on display in black and white: the charade
of posing for the political gone viral, the reality (not virtual)
of knees, necks, nooses, chains, chain-links
fencing out/fencing in,
not again but still

Or is it a bridge—narrow, grated—
not beside still waters but over
the teeming, the troubled;
waves of multitudes crossing
the deadly current not to the old
promised land of denial but
to this other side,
rocky but reclaimed—
vast, expansive, unending—
ready to till, to sow, to harvest,
even now the faint scent
of grave-strewn blossoms
beginning to resurrect
the morning breeze.

Quarantine

Apart inside,
together they stare

not at each other
but at the worn world

beyond arm's reach.
There: the child, alone,

hopscotching away her worries.
And there: the single blue jay dotting

the drab day with color.
What is no more

and what is still
keeps moving through

the familiar view. "Remember...?"
one laughs or sighs, turning

again toward the other,
together inside.

Two Hearts, Two Windows

Deconstruction

This is the heart that house built—
partitioned, scrubbed, sanitized, dipped
twice in what was, once in what will be
(if, if, if), the smell of smoke
or bread or dog or dead *(all, all, all)*
swirling too quickly from room to room,
memory to memory, settling at long last
in the dank well of the hidden cellar
from where, three stories above,
the cloistered heart listens hard
to remember the sharp
picket fence opening
or closing, the scent
and wheeze of breeze,
of before.

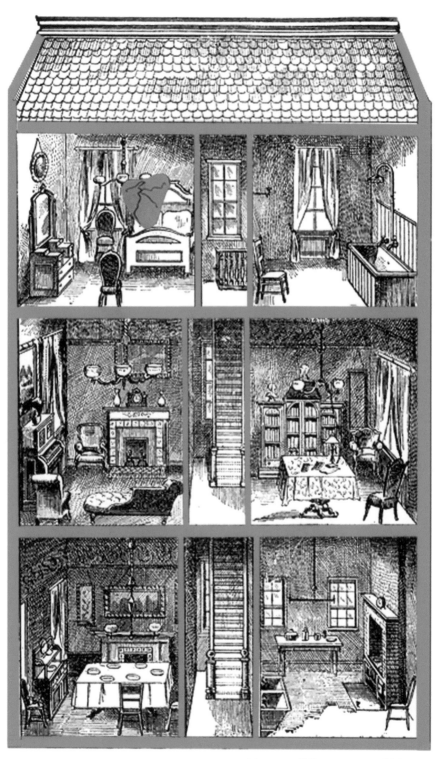

House of Quarantined Heart

Mourning Song for the Earth

Mourning Song for the Earth

Here the stone heart
waits for the tug of tide,

the undertow of pull,
the grainy *tabula rasa* of mind

lapped clean of conscience.
Or not. Even now,

seaweeds entwine; brittle
entanglements rot in the sun.

The dying snare the dead.
Such rocky shores.

Each dawn, the gulls caw
their crescendo of shriek,

capsized days breaking
into dirge, the cracked

and soulful as lonely
as this sad ballad of loss,

swooping low then rising
in morning's daily aubade of hope.

Such deceptive beauty:
elegy for the earth.

Triptych

"Fool's Gold," shimmers the leaf
letting go of Indian summer. It's on its way
to crackle but doesn't look back.

"Silver," glistens the pavement where it settles,
cracked as old parchment but fluid
in its argent-glow.

The stone itself is silent: bronze-kissed,
fissured, pock-marked paradox
of heart and all our seasons.

Heart Fall

Heart, Lichen, Stone

This is what they know:
the dip into frigid;
the shadowed shelter of cave;
the beauty of decay at dusk, at dawn;
the tattooed rays of one more orbit
of earth around a sun that says, "Hold on,
hold on, hold on." And they want to,
and they do, and they will, lingering
a little longer beneath the open branches
of forest, beside the cool stream of hope,
waiting for you, for me, for whoever
stumbles first down the long path
calling their names.

Heart Holding On

Day Is Done. Is Beginning.

Evening grays into rest:
low light, cool earth;

cushion of moss;
scent of clover or pine

that fastens the mind
to the living beneath,

around, or above
the expanding arc

of our hearts if only
we'd breathe in

the pulse and hum
of the land and the one

beside us now, reclining
like this on dirt that holds

and enfolds us in Earth's
quiet comfort of calm,

this needed rhythm
of rest/rise/repeat singing

us toward each day's
shimmering season of sleep.

Two Hearts

About the Author and Photographer

Winner of *America Magazine's* 2019 Foley Poetry Prize and Professor of English and Creative Writing at Lock Haven University, **Marjorie Maddox** has published eleven collections of poetry—including *Transplant, Transport, Transubstantiation* (Yellowglen Prize); *True, False, None of the Above* (Illumination Book Award Medalist); *Local News from Someplace Else, Perpendicular As I* (Sandstone Book Award)—the story collection *What She Was Saying* (Fomite Press); children and young adult books—*Inside Out: Poems on Writing and Reading Poems with Insider Exercises; I'm Feeling Blue, Too!; Rules of the Game: Baseball Poems; and A Crossing of Zebras: Animal Packs in Poetry—Common Wealth: Contemporary Poets on Pennsylvania* (co-editor with Jerry Wemple, Penn State University Press); *Presence: A Journal of Catholic Poetry* (assistant editor); and 650 stories, essays, and poems in journals and anthologies. Her newest collection, *Begin with a Question*, is forthcoming from Paraclete Press in 2022. **www.marjoriemaddox.com**

After teaching college English for forty years, **Karen Elias** is now an artist/activist, using photography to record the fragility of the natural world and raise awareness about climate change. Her work is in private collections, has been exhibited in several galleries, and has won numerous awards. She is a board member of the Clinton County Arts Council where she serves as membership chair and curator of the annual juried photography exhibit.

Elias and **Maddox** are engaged in an exciting, mutually inspiring project, combining poetry and photography in creative collaboration. Their work has been exhibited at The

Station Gallery (Lock Haven, Pennsylvania). Additional collaborations have appeared in such literary, arts, or medical humanities journals as *About Place: Works of Resistance and Resilience, Cold Mountain Review, The Ekphrastic Review, The Other Journal, Glint, Masque & Spectacle, Open: Journal of Arts and Letters,* and *Ars Medica.*

Shanti Arts

Nature · Art · Spirit

Please visit us online
to browse our entire book catalog,
including poetry collections and fiction,
books on travel, nature, healing, art,
photography, and more.

Also take a look at our highly regarded art
and literary journal, *Still Point Arts Quarterly*,
which may be downloaded for free.

www.shantiarts.com

CPSIA information can be obtained
at www.ICGtesting.com
Printed in the USA
BVHW020825240322
632248BV00001B/1